T0045258

Horace's Home Helpers

Sharon Holt
Illustrated by Gaston Vanzet

Contents

Chapter 1 Visiting Uncle Horace 4

Chapter 2 Amazing Inventions. 10

Chapter 3 Back to the
Drawing Board 16

Chapter 4 The Amazing Clean
Up Machine 22

Chapter 5 A Handy Invention 26

The Facts Behind the Story 30

Extend Your Reading 32

Chapter 1
Visiting Uncle Horace

Adam liked living next door to Uncle Horace. Uncle Horace spent most of his time inventing things. Adam liked to help him with his inventions.

Once Uncle Horace and Adam made a robot that brought in the mail—until its wheels fell off. In fact, Uncle Horace's inventions often fell apart, spun out of control, or exploded. But that didn't seem to worry him.

"Never mind," he would say when one of his inventions went wrong. "We'll just have to go back to the drawing board."

One day, Uncle Horace phoned Adam's house. He wanted Adam to come and see some of his new inventions.

"I'll be right over," Adam said.

But just then his mom walked into his room.

"You're not going anywhere until you've cleaned up your room," she said.

"But Mom," moaned Adam. "It's a mess."

"Exactly," said Mom. "That's why you need to clean it up."

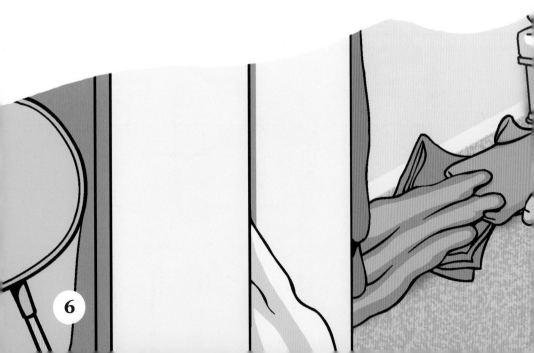

The floor was covered with clothes.
The desk was covered with books. The bed
wasn't made.

Adam threw his clothes into the closet.
He pushed other things under the bed.
He stacked his books into a big pile. Then
he kicked his soccer ball under the desk.

"There," said Adam. "That's much better."

Mom came in to check. "Well," she said.
"It's not much better, but it'll do for now. You
can finish cleaning it up when you get back."

Chapter 2
Amazing Inventions

When Adam went to Uncle Horace's house, he found him standing in the kitchen wearing things that looked like fluffy skis.

"Wow, a new invention!" exclaimed Adam.

"That's right," said Uncle Horace. "This is AFCI—my Amazing Floor Cleaning Invention." He showed Adam how to use the fluffy skis to sweep the floor.

"I didn't know sweeping the floor could be so much fun," said Adam.

"That's not all," said Uncle Horace. He slid over to the kitchen sink and attached a long plastic hose to the end of a pipe next to the sink.

"This is AMSU—my Amazing Mess Sucker Upper," he said.

11

Uncle Horace explained that AMSU sucked the mess from the floor through the hose. And the hose was connected to the trash can outside.

He pushed a button and Adam heard a loud whooshing sound. He watched as a pile of dust and fluff disappeared into the hose. The hose kept moving around the floor looking for more mess to clean up.

"That's amazing," said Adam. "I'd like to give it a try!"

Uncle Horace was showing Adam how to attach the AFCI to his shoes when the AMSU hose twisted across the floor toward them.

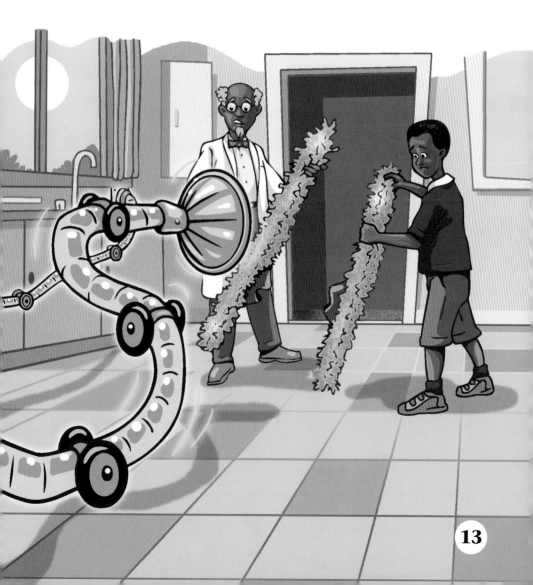

"Stand back!" said Uncle Horace, grabbing the hose and turning the switch off at the wall. "It almost sucked the shoes right off my feet when I was trying it out yesterday."

Adam slid around the floor on the fluffy AFCI skis. "I think Mom might like a pair of these to help her clean our kitchen," he said.

"I already have a purple pair wrapped up for her birthday," Uncle Horace said.

"That's good," said Adam. "But I don't think she's ready for your AMSU invention just yet."

"No," agreed Uncle Horace. "I think AMSU needs to go back to the drawing board for a few changes."

Chapter 3
Back to the Drawing Board

"All that work has made me hungry," said Uncle Horace. "Let's have a snack."

They went into the dining room and sat down at the table. Adam saw that there was nothing to eat. He asked his uncle if he should get some food from the kitchen.

"You don't have to do a thing," said Uncle Horace. "My new robot invention will bring us something to eat." He pushed a button on the table.

After a couple of minutes, a robot carrying a tray of fruit and juice rolled into the room.

"Wow!" said Adam. "That's amazing."

The robot went over to Adam and bowed. As it did, the tray tipped forward. Fruit and juice spilled all over Adam!

"Oh dear!" said Uncle Horace. "I'll take that one back to the drawing board, too. Let's get you cleaned up."

Adam and Uncle Horace went into the bathroom. Uncle Horace pulled a long hose out from the bathroom cupboard.

"We could use AMSU for this job, too," said Uncle Horace.

"No thanks, Uncle Horace," Adam said. "I think I'll just use a washcloth this time."

"Well, that would work, too," said Uncle Horace as he put the hose back.

"Have you got any more new inventions to show me?" asked Adam when he was cleaned up.

"Just one more," said Uncle Horace. They went to the workshop and Uncle Horace showed Adam the drawing board.

"This is my newest invention," he said, pointing to a drawing that looked like an octopus.

"What is it?" asked Adam.

"I call it ACUM—my Amazing Clean Up Machine," said Uncle Horace. "It does four jobs at once, two arms for each job."

"Four jobs at once!" said Adam. "That's amazing. Have you built it yet?"

"Yes, I have," answered Uncle Horace. "Come. I'll show you."

Chapter 4
The Amazing Clean Up Machine

In Uncle Horace's bedroom, a robot with eight colorful metal arms stood beside the bed.

Uncle Horace said ACUM could make the bed, hang clothes in the closet, put books on shelves, and clean up everything else.

"I need one of these myself," said Adam. "Mom's always telling me how messy my bedroom is!"

"Give it a try, then," said Uncle Horace. He handed Adam a remote control. Each pair of robot arms was colored to match a button on the remote control.

He pushed the purple button. Using its two purple arms, the robot made the bed.

Next, Adam pushed the yellow button. Two yellow arms scooped up books and put them on the shelf. Then Adam pushed the blue button. Two blue arms picked up clothes and hung them in the closet.

Finally, Adam pushed the green button. Suddenly, all the arms became tangled. Books, clothes, and blankets were thrown all over the room!

"Duck!" yelled Uncle Horace.

"How do I stop it?" shouted Adam.

"Push the red button on the back," said Uncle Horace, diving onto the floor.

Adam pressed the button and the machine stopped at last.

"Now I have a new mess to clean up," Uncle Horace said, looking around in dismay.

"Back to the drawing board again," said Adam. "But I have an idea."

Chapter 5
A Handy Invention

Back in the workshop, Adam drew something on the drawing board.

"What is it?" asked Uncle Horace.

"My Amazing Do Anything Machine," said Adam. "It has five moving parts, but it only does one job at a time."

"Can it clean up my room?" asked Uncle Horace.

"Yes," said Adam. "But it's better if you use two. Four would be even better."

"Let's start building!" said Uncle Horace.

"We don't need to," said Adam. "You already have two attached to your arms!"

Uncle Horace looked down at his hands.

"Of course," he smiled. "I don't think I can improve on that."

The two inventors went next door.

"Hello," said Mom. "Have you changed the world with your inventions yet?"

Uncle Horace laughed. "I'm going back to the drawing board to make some improvements," he said. "But Adam has come up with something that is perfect for cleaning up bedrooms. It's called the Amazing Do Anything Machine."

"I like the sound of that," said Mom. "It would be very handy to have one of those around here."

"You're right," said Adam, holding out his hands. "My ADAM invention is very handy indeed!"

Robots

Robots are machines that can move and work on their own. Some robots look like people, but they can be any shape or size. Robots can do many different jobs.

Robots in Factories

Many factories use robots. Robots can help build machines, such as cars. The robots are programmed to do certain jobs. They can do the same job over and over again, and they never get tired or bored! Robots can also do jobs that are too dangerous for people to do.

These robots are helping to make cars in a factory.

Robots at Home

Inventors have had many ideas for robots that do housework. Not many of these robots exist yet. But there are some robots that can do jobs such as cleaning floors and cutting grass. In the future, there might be robots that can cook dinner or help with homework!

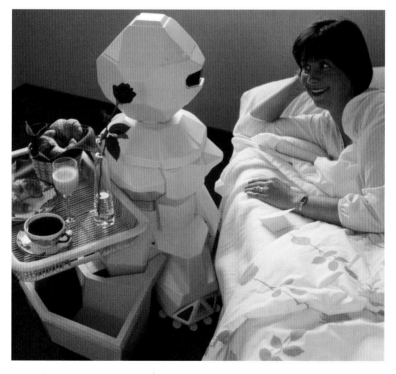

This robot helps with everyday jobs round the house.

Think About the Story

In *Horace's Home Helpers*, Uncle Horace loves to invent things and Adam loves to help him. Think about these questions.

- Sometimes Uncle Horace says he has to "go back to the drawing board." What does he mean? Why does he say this?
- What kinds of things does Uncle Horace like to invent? How helpful are his inventions?
- What is Adam's invention? Is it really an invention?

To learn more about inventions, read the books below.

SUGGESTED READING
Windows on Literacy
Time Lines: 1900–2000
Bicycles